Editor: Cliff Muehlenberg
Associate Editors: Geri Truszynski, Mike Beno
Art Director: Linda Dzik
Production Assistant: Claudia Wardius
Publisher: Roy J. Reiman

©1997 Reiman Publications, L.P.
5400 S. 60th St., Greendale, WI 53129

International Standard Book Number: 0-89821-212-X
Library of Congress Catalog Card Number: 97-65776

601
Sayings To Make You
SMILE

**A collection
of uplifting thoughts
to brighten your day.**

⊰⊱❉⊰⊱

*The sayings in this book were compil
from the pages of Country,
Country EXTRA, Reminisce and
Reminisce EXTRA magazines.*

0

6

Smile!
Golden Moments

Chapter 1

*People don't grow old;
they merely get old
by not growing.*

⸺❋⸺

*Old age is always 15 years
older than you are.*

⸺❋⸺

*Age is a high price to pay
for maturity.*

⸺❋⸺

*I'd rather wear out than
rust out.*

6

Golden Moments

*Age enables us to
recognize a mistake when
we make it again.*

*Formula for youth:
Keep your enthusiasm
and forget your birthdays.*

*You've never been as old
as you are this minute,
and you'll never be
as young again.*

Everyone wants to live long, but no one wants to grow old.

⋯⊶❀⊷⋯

Fifty is the old age of youth and the youth of old age.

⋯⊶❀⊷⋯

Age does not diminish the extreme disappointment of having a scoop of ice cream fall from the cone.

*Wrinkles should merely
indicate where smiles
have been.*

*An old-timer is a
person who's had lots
of interesting experiences,
some of them true.*

*A grouch is a person who
somehow can manage to
find something wrong even
with the good old days.*

Years wrinkle the skin,
but lack of enthusiasm
wrinkles the soul.

—✦—

"Over the hill"
means the hardest climb
is over and the view
is terrific.

—✦—

Grandchildren are God's
way of compensating us
for growing old.

Young folks ought to know that we old folks know more about being young than they do about being old.

⊹⊶⊙✦⊙⊷⊹

Setting a good example for the children takes all the fun out of middle age.

⊹⊶⊙✦⊙⊷⊹

You've reached middle age when all you exercise is caution.

Sundial: an old timer.

───❀───

By the time you decide
to look for greener
pastures, you're too old
to climb the fence.

───❀───

Middle age is when you go
all out and end up all in.

───❀───

Gray hair and wrinkles
never conceal dimples.

12

Golden Moments

You're not old until it
takes you longer to rest
than it does to get tired.

✦

Being "over the hill"
isn't so bad if the descent
isn't too rapid.

✦

Growing old is mandatory.
Growing up is optional.

✦

The heart that loves
is always young.

Spring is the time when
youth dreams and
old age remembers.

❖

You know you're getting
old when you know your
way around, but you
don't feel like going.

❖

The older the violin,
the sweeter the music.

Smile!

Kid Bits

Chapter 2

15

There is only one pretty child in the world, and every mother has it.

❖

A child is a person who can dismantle in 5 minutes the toy it took you 5 hours to put together.

❖

One of the wonders of life is just that— the wonder of life.

16

Kid Bits

A *father* is someone
who carries snapshots
where his money
used to be.

⊷⊶✦⊷⊶

A *boy* anxious to mow
the lawn is too young to.

⊷⊶✦⊷⊶

A *mother's* patience is
like a tube of toothpaste—
it's never quite all gone.

A lot of growing up takes place between "it fell" and "I dropped it".

⋯❋⋯

Children do, indeed, help hold a marriage together, keeping their parents so busy they don't have time to quarrel.

⋯❋⋯

A kindergarten teacher is someone who loves children and hates zippers.

18

Kid Bits

Children in a family are like flowers in a bouquet—there's always one that will face in the opposite direction.

❈

Most every kid says Father "no's" best.

❈

There's nothing wrong with today's teenager that 20 years won't cure.

What we need is a toy that picks itself up off the floor.

⟐

A teenager is a person who answers the phone in the middle of the first ring.

⟐

A good many childhood ailments are cured miraculously as soon as it's too late to go to school.

*People who say they
"sleep like a baby"
never had one.*

---

*There are three ways
to get things done:
do it yourself, hire
someone else to do it or
forbid your kids to do it.*

---

*Any man can be a father,
but it takes a special man
to be a dad.*

21

Kid Bits

If all your problems
are behind you, you must
be a school bus driver.

Maybe kids would eat
better if you installed a
drive-up window off the
kitchen and handed them
dinner in a bag.

By the time a man
realizes his father was
right, he has a son who
thinks he's wrong.

*For most kids, cleanliness
isn't next to godliness—
it's next to impossible.*

---

*Yes, children are
deductible. But they
also can be taxing.*

---

*Music is the sound children
make when they romp
through the house.
Noise is the sound others'
children make under
similar circumstances.*

Kid Bits

If you let your children grow without trimming their buds, don't expect many blossoms.

An unusual child is one who asks questions that his parents can answer.

No day is complete until you've heard the laughter of a child.

Smile!

Live and Learn

Chapter 3

Any philosophy that can
fit into a nutshell
belongs there.

⁕

School is a building
with four walls—and
tomorrow inside.

⁕

By the time you learn all
the lessons in life, you're
too weak to walk to the
head of the class.

Everyone I meet
knows more about
something than I do.

⇥⊙✳⊙⇤

The excuse for missing
homework used to be
"the dog ate it".
Now it's "the disk
was erased".

⇥⊙✳⊙⇤

Teachers open the doors;
you enter by yourself.

27

Live and Learn

Education is what you have left when you have lost all your notes.

⊰❀⊱

The difference between genius and stupidity is that genius has its limits.

⊰❀⊱

A simple realization that there are other points of view is the beginning of wisdom.

28

Live and Learn

*Experience is the
name everyone gives
their mistakes.*

⟶•◉•⟵

*Measure your success by
the challenges and lessons
you learn along the way.*

⟶•◉•⟵

*Education is a wonderful
thing; if you couldn't
sign your name,
you'd have to pay cash.*

One must have the right
to choose, even to choose
wrong, if he is ever to
learn to choose right.

A word to the wise
isn't as good as
a word from the wise.

Every time you graduate
from the school of
experience, someone thinks
up a new course.

*Knowledge is the train;
wisdom is the engine
that pulls it.*

⟶⟩⊙✦⊙⟨⟵

*Making mistakes
isn't stupid;
disregarding them is.*

⟶⟩⊙✦⊙⟨⟵

*You get education by
reading the fine print
...and experience
by not reading it.*

31

Live and Learn

One thorn of experience
is worth a whole wilderness
of warning.

⊷❁⊶

Anyone can make a
mistake; a fool insists on
repeating it.

⊷❁⊶

We find comfort
among those who agree
with us—growth among
those who don't.

*You may glean knowledge
by reading, but you must
separate the chaff from
the wheat by thinking.*

---

*We need to be
reminded more than we
need to be educated.*

---

*Admitting you're wrong
is like saying you're
wiser today than you
were yesterday.*

33

Live and Learn

*We learn from experience
that people seldom learn
from experience.*

※

*Don't try to learn the
tricks of the trade until
you've learned the trade.*

※

*Today's preparation
determines tomorrow's
achievement.*

34

Live and Learn

Smile!
A Friend Indeed

Chapter 4

35

A friend is the first one
to walk in when
the world walks out.

❖

A friend indeed is that
rare soul who sees
right through us,
but sees us through.

❖

A good neighbor is one
that paints his side
of your fence.

*No time is ever wasted
that makes two people
better friends.*

❈

*You can never win
simply by trying to
even the score.*

❈

*What's the use of having
an enemy if you can
have a friend.*

A cheerful friend is
like a sunny day.

⊰⊙⊱

Be wiser than other
people, if you can, but
don't tell them so.

⊰⊙⊱

Go often to the
house of your friends,
for weeds choke up
the unused path.

A good way to forget
your troubles is to
help others out of theirs.

⟶⊶❉⊷⟵

Forgiveness is the
fragrance a flower
gives off when
you step on it.

⟶⊶❉⊷⟵

Give first impressions
a second opinion.

Too many people are like porcupines—they have their good points, but you can't get near them.

―⊶❋⊷―

The biggest step you can take is when you meet others halfway.

―⊶❋⊷―

Keep good company and you will be counted among them.

So often our listening
is only in part, what we
really need is a hearing aid
for the heart.

⋯⊷✺⊶⋯

The nicest things about
new friends is they haven't
heard your old stories.

⋯⊷✺⊶⋯

We are here to see one
another through...not to
see through one another.

41

A Friend Indeed

*Stay in touch;
absence makes the heart
grow yonder.*

∗▬❋▬∗

*Good friends are
sometimes God's apology
for giving us some of our
relatives.*

∗▬❋▬∗

*A gossip talks about
others…a bore talks
about himself…a brilliant
person talks about you.*

*Forgiveness is the key
that opens the door to
freedom from resentment.*

⊷⊙❋⊙⊶

*A friend is long sought,
hardly found and
with difficulty kept.*

⊷⊙❋⊙⊶

*The one absolutely
unselfish friend a
person has in this selfish
world is his dog.*

Criticism from a
friend is better than
flattery from an enemy.

⊷⊷❀⊷⊷

People are lonely
because they build walls
instead of bridges.

⊷⊷❀⊷⊷

Quarrels would not last
long if the fault were
only on one side.

A task worth doing and
friends worth having
make life worthwhile.

⊷⊷❀⊶⊶

Never pick a quarrel,
even when it's ripe.

⊷⊷❀⊶⊶

Before you flare up
at another's faults,
take time to count 10
of your own.

No matter what scale we use, we never know the weight of another person's burden.

Friends are those who do their knocking before they enter instead of after they leave.

Empathy is your pain in my heart.

46

A Friend Indeed

Smile!

'Tis Better to Give

Chapter 5

47

Give not from the top
of your purse, but from
the bottom of your heart.

⁕

Kindness is the oil
that takes the friction
out of life.

⁕

When it comes to giving,
some people stop
at nothing.

48

'Tis Better to Give

Never put off until
tomorrow a kindness
you can do today.

--=◉=--

Learn the joy of giving,
for when you only receive
you miss much of life.

--=◉=--

The milk of human
kindness should not
be bottled up.

49

'Tis Better to Give

The reason volunteers
aren't paid is not because
they're worthless, but
because they're priceless.

❖

No one becomes dizzy
from doing good turns.

❖

The measure of life is
not its duration but
its donation.

50

'Tis Better to Give

We make a living by what
we get, but we make a life
by what we give.

—◦❂◦—

The best exercise for the
heart is to bend down
and help someone.

—◦❂◦—

Sympathy says
"I'm sorry"; compassion
says, "I'll help".

The only persons you
should want to get even
with are those who
have helped you.

Service is love in action.

There may be times
when you'll be sorry
about something…but
you'll never be sorry
that you were kind.

52

'Tis Better to Give

In this world of
give-and-take,
there are too few people
who are willing
to give what it takes.

The best way to knock
a chip off your neighbor's
shoulder is to give him
a pat on the back.

Timely good deeds are
nicer than afterthoughts.

*Giving is an exercise
that makes a healthy heart.*

⸭⸙✦⸙⸭

*When a person is down,
an ounce of help is better
than a pound of preaching.*

⸭⸙✦⸙⸭

*When someone puts
a limit on what they
will do, they put a limit
on what they can do.*

54

'Tis Better to Give

*Give of yourself…
it's the place to start…the
wallet is often too
far from the heart.*

*The hardest thing for most
people to give is…IN.*

*Do not forget little
kindnesses and do not
remember little faults.*

*Fragrance lingers on
the hands of those
who hand out roses.*

───❋───

*Politeness has been
well-defined as
benevolence in
small things.*

───❋───

*When you are good
to others, you are best
to yourself.*

Smile!
Through the Grapevine

Chapter 6

57

A word spoken is like
a sparrow—once it
flies out, you can't
catch it.

❋

Busy people don't have
time to be busybodies.

❋

The best way to spread the
most news in the least time
is to disguise it as a secret.

58

Through the Grapevine

Bless the parrot.
It repeats what it hears
without trying to
"spice it up".

The wise judge by what
they see; the foolish, by
what they hear.

Two things are bad for the
heart—running uphill
and running down people.

A gossip is a fool with
a keen sense of rumor.

⋯⊶✸⊷⋯

A secret is either
too good to keep or
it isn't worth keeping.

⋯⊶✸⊷⋯

Any faucet can turn the
water on, but after a few
years, only a good faucet
will turn it off. The same
applies to human tongues.

*There is no happiness
for people when it comes
at the expense of
other people.*

---

*Before repeating anything
a little bird told you,
be sure it wasn't a cuckoo.*

---

*It is better to bite
your tongue than to let it
bite someone else.*

61

Through the Grapevine

The truth is like
a rubber band; if you
stretch it too far, it's not
good for anything.

***

We should never
get caught in our own
mouthtrap.

***

A gossip is the
knife of the party.

You cannot be envious and happy at the same time.

⸺✦⸺

Gossip is remembered long after good deeds are forgotten.

⸺✦⸺

One reason a dog is a good friend may be because it wags its tail and not its tongue.

Some people are
like buttons, always
popping off.

⊰⊱

You can speak to the point
without being sharp.

⊰⊱

Gossip is like mud thrown
against a clean wall.
It may not stick, but it
leaves a mark.

I can keep a secret…but
those I tell it to never can.

⊷⊙❂⊙⊶

A mistake proves someone
stopped talking long
enough to do something.

⊷⊙❂⊙⊶

Keeping a secret from
some people is like trying
to sneak daylight
past a rooster.

Some people have eyes
that see not and ears that
hear not, but never
tongues that talk not.

⊷⊙⊶

The great trouble with
an idle rumor is it
doesn't remain so.

⊷⊙⊶

He who sows thorns
should never go barefoot.

66

Through the Grapevine

Smile!

Happiness Is...

Chapter 7

67

We may be sure we are
not pleasing God if we
are not happy ourselves.

───◦❁◦───

Vacations would be a lot
more pleasant if you could
stop the lawn along with
the paper and mail.

───◦❁◦───

A smile is the carnation in
the buttonhole of life.

*Happiness held is
a seed…happiness shared
is a flower.*

*A cloudy day is no match
for a sunny disposition.*

*A warm smile and
wholesome laughter have
great face value.*

69

Happiness Is…

Be happy with what you
have and who you are;
be generous with both,
and you won't have to
hunt for happiness.

❖

Happiness is an inside job.

❖

May it matter not
that we are stars,
but that we twinkle.

70

Happiness Is…

*Happiness is living each
day as though it were the
first day of a marriage and
the last day of vacation.*

⊰═◉❈◎═⊱

*The sunshine of life
is made up of very little
beams that are bright
all the time.*

⊰═◉❈◎═⊱

*A laugh is a smile
that bursts.*

71

Happiness Is...

*Happiness is one thing
that multiplies by division.*

---

*The gift of happiness
belongs to those who
unwrap it.*

---

*Genuine elation comes
when you feel you could
touch a star without
standing on tiptoe.*

Happiness Is...

The world looks brighter
from behind a smile.

Get happiness out of your
work, or you may never
know what happiness is.

Great mountains of
happiness grow out of
little hills of kindness.

73

Happiness Is...

*Good humor is the
health of the soul.*

---

*It isn't our position
but our disposition that
makes us happy.*

---

*The best way to cheer
yourself up is to try to
cheer somebody else up.*

---

*Unshared joy is
an unlighted candle.*

74

Happiness Is...

Happiness is a
conscious choice, not an
automatic response.

✦

Joy is the echo
of God's life in us.

✦

Between each dawn and
setting sun, set aside
some time for fun.

✦

A smile goes a long way,
but usually comes back.

75

Happiness Is...

All who find joy
must share it; happiness
was born a twin.

⊷⊷❀⊷⊷

We all can't be shining
examples, but we can all
twinkle a little.

⊷⊷❀⊷⊷

Happiness is not so much
in having as in sharing.

⊷⊷❀⊷⊷

Let your light shine with
love, service and a smile.

76

Happiness Is...

*Enjoy life…this is not
a dress rehearsal.*

⋅⇥⫸⊷✿⊶⫷⇤⋅

*It's important to make
someone happy every day,
even if it's just yourself.*

⋅⇥⫸⊷✿⊶⫷⇤⋅

*The city of happiness
is located in the
state of mind.*

⋅⇥⫸⊷✿⊶⫷⇤⋅

*Praise is the soil in which
joy thrives.*

77

Happiness Is…

*Three essentials of
happiness are something
to do, someone to love and
something to hope for.*

───❀───

*Never miss an opportunity
to make someone happy.*

───❀───

*Yesterday is gone;
tomorrow is a gamble;
today is a sure thing—
make the most of it.*

78

Happiness Is...

Smile!

Just for Laughs

Chapter 8

79

The difference between
looking good and
good-looking is 20 years
and 20 pounds.

———✳———

When playing golf,
if you can't be good,
at least be quick.

———✳———

Common sense is just
about the most
uncommon thing there is.

When a man is singing
in the shower, it means
the kids didn't use up
all the water.

⟖═◉✿◉═⟕

Willpower is the ability
to eat one salted peanut.

⟖═◉✿◉═⟕

When a resort owner
insists they're biting,
make sure he's talking
about fish, not mosquitoes.

When the wife is on the warpath, you can expect a call to active duty.

⋯⦿⋯

You can always recall moving an item to a "safer place", but never recall where that place is.

⋯⦿⋯

The exclamation point may become obsolete. No one is surprised at anything anymore.

*You can't be fit as a fiddle
when you're
tight as a drum.*

*Why is it always the driver
in the third car in line
who's the first to see
the light change?*

*When asked to plant a
garden, the first thing
many people dig up
is an excuse.*

When you are up
to your ears in trouble,
try using the part
that isn't submerged.

⊷⊷❈⊶⊶

Closets are something
some people hang things
in when they run out
of doorknobs.

⊷⊷❈⊶⊶

Christmas would be much
nicer if elves assembled
ALL the toys.

*Where one generation
begins and another one
ends is about
11 o'clock at night.*

—◦◦❀◦◦—

*When high school kids
wear rags today,
we call it self-expression.
When I was young and
dressed this way, we called
it the Depression.*

—◦◦❀◦◦—

*Nothing is interesting
if you're not interested.*

Why hire someone with a
divining rod to find water
when a kid with new shoes
will do it for free?

❈

You can pull on a duck's
neck all you want,
but you're still not going
to come up with a swan.

❈

One way to get ahead
and stay ahead is to
use your head.

"In the nick of time" is an expression invented by a man who overslept one morning and had to shave in a hurry.

A vacationer caught a fish so big he dislocated both shoulders describing it.

Childish games: those at which your spouse beats you.

A word of wisdom is often like a worm in a cornfield—it goes in one ear and out the other.

You know it's going to be a bad day when your twin forgets your birthday.

We'll never know what an average person thinks until we can find one who will admit he's average.

88

Smile!

Love Conquers All

Chapter 9

89

*You maintain a house
with paint and plaster;
you maintain a home
with love.*

❈

*The riches that are in the
heart can never be stolen.*

❈

*Time endears but
cannot fade the memories
that love has made.*

90

Love Conquers All

*In labors of love,
every day is payday.*

---

*Three things make us
content: the seeing eye,
the hearing ear,
the responsive heart.*

---

*Nobody has ever
measured how much
the heart can hold.*

You may give without loving, but you can't love without giving.

When love adorns the home, other decorations are secondary.

Only love can be divided endlessly and still not diminish.

Given with love,
a fistful of dandelions
means as much
as a dozen roses.

⟞⟐⟝

Let there be space
in your togetherness.

⟞⟐⟝

Put a little more love in
living, and you will love
life more than ever before.

Teach your hands to help
and your heart to love.

—◦❋◦—

Love enriches;
it doesn't rehabilitate.

—◦❋◦—

Kindness in words
creates confidence;
kindness in thinking
creates profoundness;
kindness in giving
creates love.

Love Conquers All

*Faults are thick
where love is thin.*

---

*What's stitched with love
will never tear.*

---

*The heart holds things
the mind forgets.*

---

*Love is always an
appropriate gift.*

95

Love Conquers All

When there is love
in the home,
there is joy in the heart.

❈

The heart has its reasons
which reason does not
understand.

❈

Real love stories
never have endings.

❈

We pardon
as long as we love.

96

Love Conquers All

A house is built by human hands, but a home is built by human hearts.

Smoke pouring out from a chimney reminds me of a house full of love.

Marriages may be made in heaven, but the details have to be worked out here on earth.

97

Love Conquers All

*If your heart is full of love,
you always have
something to give.*

⊰❀⊱

*As perfume is to the
flower, kindness is to
speech.*

⊰❀⊱

*Hold those you love
with open hands.*

Smile! You Can Do It!

Chapter 10

99

*Some folks may succeed
because they're
destined to, but most
succeed because they're
determined to.*

✦

*Defeat never comes to any
man until he admits it.*

✦

*Life involves tearing up
one rough draft after
another.*

*It's not so important
where we are standing
but in what direction
we are moving.*

———❊———

*Obstacles are what you see
when you take your eyes
off the goal.*

———❊———

*Be not afraid of moving
slowly; be afraid
of standing still.*

101

You Can Do It!

The surest way to get
somewhere is to know
where you are going.

<hr />

If the wind doesn't blow,
row.

<hr />

Things may come
to those who wait,
but only the things left
by those who hustle.

Success is a journey,
not a destination.

⊷⊚❀⊚⊶

A lot of us would like
to move mountains,
but few of us are willing
to practice on small hills.

⊷⊚❀⊚⊶

The future belongs
to those who create it.

103

You Can Do It!

Coming together
is a beginning;
keeping together
is progress;
staying together
is success.

✦

Do your best today;
tomorrow will be easier.

✦

Don't let yesterday use
up too much of today.

104

You Can Do It!

Don't waste time
reflecting on where
to start; just start.

―――❀―――

Having the right aim in life
isn't enough if you
run out of ammunition.

―――❀―――

If something was
worth doing, then you've
already been paid.

105
You Can Do It!

*If you don't know
where you are going,
you have already arrived.*

---

*If you never have a dream,
you will never have
a dream come true.*

---

*If you want to leave
footprints in the
sands of time,
don't drag your feet.*

You Can Do It!

Look forward
to some success,
not backward
to any failure.

Success has a simple
formula—do your best,
and people may like it.

You may be disappointed
if you fail, but you are
doomed if you don't try.

107

You Can Do It!

*Always give 100% and
you'll never have to
second-guess yourself.*

⊷✺⊶

*Success comes from what
you think, not what you
think you ought to do.*

⊷✺⊶

*The future belongs
to those who create it.*

108

You Can Do It!

Smile!

Memorable Moments

Chapter 11

109

A good snapshot
stops a moment
from running away.

✦

Cherish all your happy
moments; they make
a fine cushion for old age.

✦

Memories are keepsakes
of the happy times
we've known.

*Home is where you hang
your memories.*

⋯⊷◉✺◉⊶⋯

*Past experience
should be a guidepost,
not a hitching post.*

⋯⊷◉✺◉⊶⋯

*Remember when people
who did windows included
gas station attendants?*

*We are part of the
same story, as long as
one of us is still around
to remember.*

⟿⊙✿⊙⟿

*What we keep in memory
is ours, unchanged forever.*

⟿⊙✿⊙⟿

*Recall it as often as you
wish—a happy memory
never wears out.*

Memory is the diary
we all carry with us.

To understand a man,
you must understand
his memories.

You can clutch the past so
tightly that it leaves your
arms too full to embrace
the present.

113

Memorable Moments

We do not remember days;
we remember moments.

———❀———

Memories shared are
blessings that
keep on giving.

———❀———

One of the best gifts you
can give your children
is good memories.

Remember when the only tanning parlor in town was the woodshed?

⊷⊶⊷✦⊶⊷⊶

To better the future, know the past.

⊷⊶⊷✦⊶⊷⊶

Without the past, neither the present nor future could exist.

We can improve our
tomorrows with a better
understanding of
our yesterdays.

∗⊰❈⊱∗

Nostalgia is the sandpaper
that removes the
rough edges from the
good old days.

∗⊰❈⊱∗

No day is over
if it makes a memory.

116

Memorable Moments

Remember when the star athlete's only compensation was a letter sweater?

—✦—

The moment may be temporary, but the memory is forever.

—✦—

We cannot lose our faith in the future without first losing our memory of the past.

117

Memorable Moments

You never know when
you're making a memory.

⟶⊶✦⊷⟵

The real measure of
your wealth is how much
you'd be worth if you
lost all your money.

⟶⊶✦⊷⟵

Today is the day
to make memories.

Chapter 12

*Every man is the architect
of his own fortune.*

---

*Watch the pennies, and
the dollars will take care
of themselves.*

---

*When you get something
for nothing, you just
haven't been billed yet.*

In the good old days,
people who saved
money were considered to
be misers. Now
they're considered
miracle workers.

—◦◦❋◦◦—

Know the value of what
you're worth…
never discount it or
mark it down.

Some debts are fun when you are acquiring them, but none are fun when you are retiring them.

The person who first said "spend" your vacation never knew how right he was.

He who wants little always has enough.

Though no one can
go back and make a
brand-new start, anyone
can start from now and
make a brand-new end.

A penny for your thoughts
is now a quarter.

Debts are the certain
outcome of an
uncertain income.

123

Where Your Treasure Lies

One measure of
civilization's progress is
the way the cost of relaxing
keeps going up.

A vacation is a holiday
away from everything
but expenses.

If you want to stay out
of debt, act your wage.

Where Your Treasure Lies

A borrower is a person who wants to live within your means.

───❄───

It used to be a fool and his money were soon parted. Now it happens to everybody.

───❄───

Enthusiasm is the yeast that raises a lot of dough.

Where Your Treasure Lies

If you want to feel rich,
just count all the things
that money can't buy.

Variety may be the spice
of life, but monotony
buys the groceries.

Yesterday's nest egg will
hardly buy today's
birdhouse.

126

Where Your Treasure Lies

Smile!
Opportunity's Knocking

Chapter 13

*Opportunity doesn't
come—it has
always been there.*

*We are all faced with a
series of great opportunities
brilliantly disguised as
impossible situations.*

*Great opportunities to help
others seldom come,
but small ones
surround us daily.*

If the worst that can happen has happened, cheer up…it's the worst that can happen.

⟞⟞◉✦◉⟝⟝

Even if I knew the world was going to end tomorrow, I would plant a tree today.

⟞⟞◉✦◉⟝⟝

Faith is the bird that sings while it is still dark.

129

Opportunity's Knocking

Opportunists
knock on would.

⟶✦⟵

Problems are only
opportunities with
thorns on them.

⟶✦⟵

An optimist stays up 'til
morning to see the
New Year in. A pessimist
stays up to make sure
the old one leaves.

When opportunity knocks,
a pessimist complains
about the noise.

An optimist is one who
fastens his seat belt before
trying to start his car
on a cold winter morning.

Delightful things are
all around, simply waiting
to be found.

131

Opportunity's Knocking

Is the opportunity fraught
with difficulty or the
difficulty fraught with
opportunity?

———◈———

Opportunity is not
a lengthy visitor.

———◈———

An optimist is one who
makes the best of it when
he gets the worst of it.

132

Opportunity's Knocking

*Never cry so loud about
your hard luck that
you can't hear
opportunity knocking.*

*The optimist is as often
wrong as the pessimist,
but he is much happier.*

*The sun is always
shining somewhere.*

When things go wrong,
don't go with them.

—◦◊◦—

No opportunity is ever
lost. Someone else seizes
the ones you missed.

—◦◊◦—

The pessimist finds
the worst in the best;
the optimist discovers
the best in the worst.

134

Opportunity's Knocking

Smile!

In His Hands

Chapter 14

135

An early-morning walk
is a blessing for
the whole day.

✦

If you can't take
God with you,
don't go.

✦

Nobody has so little that
there is no room for praise,
or so much that there
is no need for prayer.

*Put your will in neutral
so that God can shift you.*

---

*Tears are God's way of
melting a heart that is
frozen with grief.*

---

*The trouble with reaching
a crossroads in life
is the lack of signposts.*

137

In His Hands

We work so hard
to keep our outside
presentable when the
inside is what matters.

❖

Be careful how you live.
You may be the only Bible
some people read.

❖

If God sends a storm, He
will also steer the vessel.

*Don't pray for rain
if you're going to complain
about the mud.*

---

*Faith does for living what
sunshine does for
stained-glass windows.*

---

*Forget the troubles
that passed away, but
remember the blessings
that come each day.*

God put a tear in your eye
so that you could see
a rainbow.

❈

If you hem in both ends
of your day with a prayer,
it won't be so likely to
unravel in the middle.

❈

When you meet
temptation, turn
to the right.

*You'll never get
the busy signal on the
prayer line to heaven.*

<hr />

*As long as there are
final exams, there will be
prayer in school.*

<hr />

*Put everything in God's
hand and eventually you
will see God's hand
in everything.*

Only God is in a position
to look down on anyone.

※

Some people treat their
religion like a spare tire—
they never expect to use it
except in an emergency.

※

God gives us the
ingredients for our daily
bread, but He expects
us to do the baking.

142

In His Hands

*Be such a person that,
if all were like you,
this world would be
paradise.*

---

*Every evening I turn my
worries over to God—
He's going to be up all
night anyway.*

---

*Every man must walk in
the garden of his soul.*

143

In His Hands

Get on your knees
and thank God you're
on your feet.

—◈—

I know not what the
future holds, but I know
who holds the future.

—◈—

Good words and good
deeds keep life's garden
free of weeds.

*Where we go hereafter
depends on what we
go after here.*

⊷⊶

*Blessed are the flexible,
for they shall not be
bent out of shape.*

⊷⊶

*God will either lighten
your load or strengthen
your back.*

145

In His Hands

He who is thankful
for little things
enjoys much.

❖

Get your soul in tune
with God before the
concert of the day begins.

❖

If you aren't as close to
God as you once were,
make no mistake about
who moved.

Smile!

Take Another Look

Chapter 15

147

*Nothing is really lost;
it's just where it
doesn't belong.*

✦

*What we must decide is
how we are valuable rather
than how valuable we are.*

✦

*Judge people from where
they stand, not from where
you stand.*

Maybe people should swap problems. Everyone, it seems, knows how to solve the other guy's.

There is always a little boy in the old man gone fishing.

If it looks cloudy, maybe your windows need washing.

149

Take Another Look

*Unless you're the lead dog,
the scenery never changes.*

❊

*Tolerance is seeing things
with your heart instead
of with your eyes.*

❊

*There is no such thing
as a weed, only a flower
that is misplaced.*

The right to do something
does not mean that
doing it is right.

✦

A hometown is where
the great are small and
the small are great.

✦

Over every mountain is
a path that can't be seen
from the valley.

Some things are loved
because they are valuable;
others are valuable
because they are loved.

When nothing can be
done about a problem,
you've overlooked
something.

There is no room at the top
for those who ought to
start near the bottom.

When you have to swallow
your own medicine,
the spoon always seems
about three times as big.

⊶⊸✦⊷⊶

If a man sees two sides of
a problem, he doesn't have
money invested in it.

⊶⊸✦⊷⊶

Instead of putting others
in their place, put yourself
in their place.

153

Take Another Look

*Originality is the art
of remembering what
you hear but forgetting
where you heard it.*

---

*When you point a finger
at someone, you are
pointing three at yourself.*

---

*People whose manners are
on the absent side are
probably missing more
than just their manners.*

154

Take Another Look

One of the most
complicated tasks modern
man faces is trying to
figure out how to
lead a simple life.

⋯⊙❂⊙⋯

It's always a good idea to
seek the advice of others,
but that doesn't mean
you have to take it.

⋯⊙❂⊙⋯

The know-it-all knows
what to do until
it happens to him.

Everything has beauty—
but not everyone sees it.

✦

If you are not part of
the solution, you are part
of the problem.

✦

It is better to look ahead
and prepare than to
look back and regret.

156

Take Another Look

Chapter 16

Never let the seeds
keep you from enjoying
the watermelon.

A man convinced
against his will is of
the same opinion still.

Advice is what we ask for
when we already know the
answer but wish we didn't.

Attitudes are contagious.
Is yours worth catching?

⟶⊙❂⊙⟵

Compliments are like
perfume—to be inhaled,
not swallowed.

⟶⊙❂⊙⟵

Humility is that elusive
thing that, the moment
you think you have it,
you've lost it.

*It takes backbone
not wishbone to
make success.*

❋

*Every idea has its
doubters; every
accomplishment, its critics.*

❋

*Some people think it's
holding on that makes
one strong…sometimes
it's letting go.*

*The purpose of existence
is not to make a living
but to make a life.*

*There is very little
difference between a man
who knows it all and a
man who knows nothing.*

---

*To know how to refuse
is as important as
to know how to consent.*

We live our lives forward
but understand them
backward.

⊷⊶✺⊷⊶

What makes you tick
sometimes needs
rewinding.

⊷⊶✺⊷⊶

With two eyes and one
tongue, you should see
twice as much as you say.

162

*You can't control
the length of your life,
but you can control
the width and depth.*

---

*A man becomes wise
by watching what
happens when he isn't.*

---

*Don't try to sweep
someone else's porch until
your own is clean.*

163

Words Worth Remembering

Home is where
you are treated best
and grumble most.

⊷❖⊶

Peace of mind is not
the absence of conflict
from life, but the ability
to cope with it.

⊷❖⊶

If you stumble twice
over the same stone,
you deserve to fall.

*It isn't necessary to blow
out the other person's light
to let your own shine.*

---

*Life is like a piano—what
you get out of it depends
on how you play it.*

---

*Maybe the reason so many
folks have their backs
to the wall is that they
have been putting up
too much of a front.*

The most important ability
is availability.

⋯⊷❖⊶⋯

When the truth is in
your way, you are
on the wrong road.

⋯⊷❖⊶⋯

A man can fail
many times, but he isn't
a failure until he begins
to blame someone else.

166
Words Worth Remembering

Smile!

What's in a Word?

Chapter 17

167

Words are the hummingbirds of the imagination.

❖

Talk is cheap…mostly because the supply is greater than the demand.

❖

When you talk you only hear what you already know.

They're easily,
thoughtlessly said.
Yet hard words can enter
the heart and lie there
as heavy as lead.

❈

Words fall lightly as snow.

❈

It takes two to speak
the truth, one to speak,
another to hear.

There is nothing as nice
as a cheerful word
of greeting.

~·≈✦≈·~

Wisdom is knowing
when to speak your mind
and when to mind
your speech.

~·≈✦≈·~

Kind words are short
to speak, but their echoes
are endless.

*A wise person knows
where free speech ends
and cheap talk begins.*

—❊—

*To communicate is
the beginning of
understanding.*

—❊—

*Don't speak unless you can
improve on the silence.*

The oldest, shortest words—"yes" and "no"—are those which require the most thought.

⊷❈⊶

A lie will travel a thousand miles while truth is putting on its boots.

⊷❈⊶

Swallowing angry words is much better than having to eat them.

172

What's in a Word?

Better to remain silent
and be thought a fool
than to open one's mouth
and remove all doubt.

❖

Even a fish wouldn't
get in trouble if he kept
his mouth shut.

❖

There is nothing in words
unless they are properly
strung together.

173

What's in a Word?

Speaking two languages
is valuable, but keeping
silent in one is precious.

※

A compliment is
verbal sunshine.

※

What should not be heard
by little ears should not be
said by big mouths.

When you hold a
conversation, don't forget
to let go once in a while.

One thing you can give
and still keep is your word.

The heart of a fool is in
his mouth, but the
mouth of a wise man is in
his heart.

What's in a Word?

A speech is like a wheel—
the longer the spoke
the greater the tire.

If something goes without
saying, it's best to let it.

It is possible to make a
sound argument without
making a lot of noise.

Smile!
Perfect Timing

Chapter 18

177

Today turns a new page
in the history of your life.

* * *

Moments are little pockets
of time that are crammed
with all of life's
possibilities.

* * *

A minute is a little thing,
but minutes make the day.
So crowd in some kind
deeds before it slips away.

*It isn't what you know
that counts; it's what you
think of in time.*

⟶⊸✦⊷⟵

*Don't you just love
those winter mornings
when you don't have to
get up at the crack of dawn
to see the sunrise?*

⟶⊸✦⊷⟵

*Don't criticize the rooster.
If you got up at 4 a.m.,
you'd crow, too.*

179

God made time
but man made haste.
—Irish proverb

꘎

I'm not afraid of
tomorrow, for I have seen
yesterday and I love today.

꘎

The man of the hour is
the person who rarely
watches the clock.

What most people want
for Christmas is 2 more
weeks to prepare for it.

Pick your rut carefully,
as you may be in it for
a long time.

Lose an hour in the
morning and you will be
all day hunting it.

At the rate changes are occurring everywhere, anyone nostalgic for the "good old days" is yearning for last week.

—⟡—

Daylight Saving Time is like cutting off one end of a blanket and sewing it on the other end.

—⟡—

The time to relax is when you don't have the time.

182

Perfect Timing

*Life is no better
if we worry; life is no
better if we hurry.*

⋅⊶⊙✳⊙⊷⋅

*Retirement is when
the alarm clock is
no longer alarming.*

⋅⊶⊙✳⊙⊷⋅

*There should be a better
reward for promptness
than having to wait
for everyone else.*

183

Perfect Timing

A split second: the time
between the lights changing
and the driver behind you
honking his horn.

Life is like an exciting
book, and every year
starts a new chapter.

You can't turn back
the clock. But you can
wind it up again.

You will always
find time for that which
you place first.

⊰⊱

Most people spend a lot
of time dreaming about
the future, never realizing
a little arrives each day.

⊰⊱

He who watches
the clock often remains
one of the hands.

A true test of patience
is not minding
being put on hold.

The thread that knits
the movement into a
living pattern is change.

With every rising of
the sun, think of your life
as just begun.

Why is it the person with an hour to kill usually spends it with someone who can't spare a minute?

Don't put off enjoyment—there's no time like the pleasant.

Instead of counting the days, make the days count.

Take a lesson from
the clock—it passes time
by keeping its hands busy.

⋯◦❋◦⋯

Time is the wages of life;
invest it, don't spend it.

⋯◦❋◦⋯

We all need time alone:
to think, to dream,
to wonder.

Smile!
Working Works

Chapter 19

189

He who considers his
work beneath him
will be doing it well.

It's not how many
hours you put in,
but what you put in
the hours that counts.

Motivation is putting work
clothes on your dreams.

190

Working Works

*The factory that produces
the most important
product is the home.*

---

*Nothing is impossible
for the man who doesn't
have to do it himself.*

---

*A man who is waiting
for something to
turn up should start
with his own sleeves.*

191

Working Works

The difficult we do today;
the impossible takes
a little longer.

＊

Those who roll up
their sleeves seldom
lose their shirts.

＊

People get the most
tired when they are
standing still.

192

Working Works

Some people think they're
overworked because
it takes them all day
to do a half day's work.

⊷⊷⊛⊷⊷

The person who wakes up
and finds himself a success
hasn't been asleep.

⊷⊷⊛⊷⊷

Every calling is great
when greatly pursued.

*If you don't know
how to do something,
start anyway…within 5
minutes, someone will
tell you that you're
doing it wrong.*

⟶⊷❀⊶⟵

*Ask God's blessings on
your work, but don't ask
Him to do it for you.*

⟶⊷❀⊶⟵

*TEAM —Together Each
Accomplishes More.*

*It isn't the mountains
ahead that wear you out;
it's the grain of sand
in your shoe.*

—⊛—

*Work is work only
when you'd rather be
doing something else.*

—⊛—

*The bee that gets
the honey doesn't hang
around the hive.*

*Don't only do what
you like to do, but learn
to like what has
to be done.*

⟶⊷◉⊶⟵

*A diamond is a piece of
coal that stuck to its job.*

⟶⊷◉⊶⟵

*Ideas are funny little
things…they won't work
unless you do.*

It's not the load
that breaks you down,
it's the way you carry it.

Most footprints on the
sands of time were made
with work shoes.

No rule of success
will work if you don't.

197

Working Works

*One disadvantage with
having nothing to do
is you can't stop and rest.*

※

*The best way to appreciate
your job is to imagine
yourself without it.*

※

*There won't be time to
dwell in the past if
we keep busy today.*

You can't raise much
of anything if you don't
raise a little sweat.

⟡

Some people are like
blisters. They don't
show up until
the work is done.

⟡

The reward of a thing
well done is having done it.

*The greatest reward
for doing is the
opportunity to do more.*

⁂

*Common sense is genius
dressed in working clothes.*

⁂

*The best thing a man
can put in his crop or
his kids is his own shadow.*

200
Working Works

Chapter 20

201

Worry is duress rehearsal.

———❈———

Nothing lasts forever—
not even your troubles.

———❈———

You don't get an ulcer
from what you eat,
you get an ulcer
from what is eating you.

———❈———

Don't worry; be happy.

Of all our troubles,
great or small,
the greatest are those
that don't
happen at all.

Trouble knocked on
the door, heard a laugh
and turned away.

It is not work that
kills man, it is worry.

203

Why Worry?

*Worry doesn't empty
tomorrow of its problems;
it simply empties today
of its strength.*

*Keep your fears to
yourself, but share your
courage with others.*

*Don't trouble trouble,
till it troubles you.*

204

Why Worry?

Worry pulls tomorrow's cloud over today's sunshine.

✻

We should spend more time thinking of a solution and less thinking about the problem.

✻

Most problems could be solved in the time spent worrying about them.

Worry is
today's mouse eating
tomorrow's cheese.

⟶⊷✦⊶⟵

When a pessimist has
nothing to worry about,
he worries about why
he has nothing to
worry about.

⟶⊷✦⊶⟵

Most of our worries
are reruns.

If you trust,
you don't worry;
if you worry,
you don't trust.

⊷═◉❈◉═⊶

Blessed is the person
who is too busy to worry
in the daytime and too
sleepy to worry at night.

⊷═◉❈◉═⊶

Wrinkled with care
and worry? Get your
faith lifted.

207

Why Worry?

*Real difficulties
can be overcome; it's the
imaginary ones that
are unconquerable.*

---

*Worry is the
interest paid by those
who borrow trouble.*

---

*You're only cooking up
trouble when you stew
about tomorrow.*

Most of the mountains
we climb in life
we build ourselves.

—————✦—————

Worried about tomorrow?
You did that yesterday
about today.

—————✦—————

Worry is nothing more
than a mental picture
of something that
you don't want to happen.

209

Why Worry?

*Solutions occur when
we think things out;
worries occur when
we think things in.*

⊷✦⊶

*Half of what you worry
about never happens…
and the other half
happens for the best.*

210

Why Worry?

Smile!

Potpourri

Chapter 21

211

*Don't let the urgent crowd
out the important.*

---

*Even when the fabric
of peace is carefully
woven, a few scraps
are always left over.*

---

*If you don't take care
of your body, where else
are you going to live?*

*Life's heaviest burden
is to have nothing
to carry.*

---

*Many of us are more
capable than some of
us…but none of us is as
capable as all of us.*

Peace is the world smiling.

*Freedom is not the right to
do as you please, but the
liberty to do as you ought.*

———❖———

*The right temperature
at home is maintained
by warm hearts,
not by hot heads.*

———❖———

*When you feel terrific,
notify your face.*

*A grudge is one thing
that does not get better
when it is nursed.*

---

*As long as we are
changing, we are living.*

---

*If the world is cold,
make it your business
to build fires.*

215

*If you live by the calendar,
your days are numbered.*

*Sleep on what you plan
to do. Don't stay awake
over what you have done.*

*Some people have a
thousand thoughts...others
have the same thoughts
a thousand times.*

216

Potpourri

The roots grow deep when
the winds blow strong.

＊

You are most efficient
when you deliberately
forget what is
unimportant.

＊

Without courage, all other
virtues lose their meaning.

217

Potpourri

Wiser is the wisdom
that is hard won.

—⊷❀⊶—

Wouldn't it be nice to be
as sure of anything as some
people are of everything.

—⊷❀⊶—

Birds of a feather may
flock together, but eagles
soar high on their own.

*In still waters are the
largest fish.*

*Put on a smile…
one size fits all.*

*At the beginning of
the new year, we have
another chance to carve
a beautiful shape in our
own landscape.*

Turn that frown
upside down!

⁛

Driver's licenses do not
revoke walking privileges.

⁛

If we are to make a
difference in others' lives,
we have to meet them
where they are.

⁛

The easiest way to improve
your luck is to stop betting.

Contentment is
contagious.

⸰⟶⊙✦⊙⟵⸰

It's not that nice guys
finish last. Nice guys
are winners before
the game even starts.

⸰⟶⊙✦⊙⟵⸰

The most effective water
power in the world is tears.

⸰⟶⊙✦⊙⟵⸰

Always take hold of things
with a smooth handle.

221

You can't get to the end
of something until you get
to the middle of it.

❈

A seedling must weather
many a storm before
it becomes an oak.

❈

Honesty once pawned
is never redeemed.

❈

Choice, not chance,
determines destiny.

If you're green with envy,
you're ripe for trouble.

⭐

Nature creates wonders
that science only
contemplates.

⭐

Use it up, wear it out,
make it do or do without.

⭐

Better to be square than to
move in the wrong circles.

223

Potpourri

Some people get up
and go to the window
and shout,
"Good morning, Lord!"
Others pull the sheet over
their heads and say,
"Good Lord,
it's morning!"

━◦◦❁◦◦━

A pint of example is
worth a gallon of advice.

*The best thing about spring
is that it comes when it is
most needed.*

—=◉=—

*Frustration: The same
snow that covers the ski
slopes makes the roads
to them impassable.*

—=◉=—

*When you depart, leave
a vacuum, not a wake.*

225

Potpourri

*Every man is the architect
of his own fortunes, but
the neighbors superintend
the construction.*

⊷⊷❀⊶⊶

*An error is like a leak in
the roof —the amount of
damage it can do depends
on how fast you fix it.*

⊷⊷❀⊶⊶

*Life is short,
eat dessert first.*